MOVIE FAVORITES

Solos and Band Arrangements
Correlated with Essential Elements Band Method

Arranged by
MICHAEL SWEENEY

Welcome to Essential Elements Movie Favorites! There are two versions of each selection in this versatile book. The SOLO version appears on the left-hand page of your book. The FULL BAND arrangement appears on the right-hand page. Optional accompaniment recordings are available separately in CD or cassette format. Use these recordings when playing solos for friends and family.

ISBN 978-0-7935-5975-6

HAL•LEONARD™
CORPORATION
7777 W. BLUEMOUND RD. P.O. BOX 13819 MILWAUKEE, WI 53213

From The Universal Motion Picture JURASSIC PARK

Theme From "Jurassic Park"

E♭ ALTO SAXOPHONE
Solo

Composed by JOHN WILLIAMS
Arranged by MICHAEL SWEENEY

00860029

MCA music publishing

Theme from "Jurassic Park"

E♭ **ALTO SAXOPHONE**
Band Arrangement

Composed by JOHN WILLIAMS
Arranged by MICHAEL SWEENEY

 music publishing

From CHARIOTS OF FIRE
CHARIOTS OF FIRE

E♭ ALTO SAXOPHONE
Solo

Music by VANGELIS
Arranged by MICHAEL SWEENEY

00860029

From CHARIOTS OF FIRE
CHARIOTS OF FIRE

E♭ ALTO SAXOPHONE
Band Arrangement

Music by VANGELIS
Arranged by MICHAEL SWEENEY

00860029

From THE MAN FROM SNOWY RIVER

THE MAN FROM SNOWY RIVER

(Main Title Theme)

E♭ ALTO SAXOPHONE
Solo

By BRUCE ROWLAND
Arranged by MICHAEL SWEENEY

00860029

THE MAN FROM SNOWY RIVER

(Main Title Theme)

E♭ ALTO SAXOPHONE
Band Arrangement

By BRUCE ROWLAND
Arranged by MICHAEL SWEENEY

From The Paramount Motion Picture FORREST GUMP

FORREST GUMP - MAIN TITLE

(Feather Theme)

Eb ALTO SAXOPHONE
Solo

Music by ALAN SILVESTRI
Arranged by MICHAEL SWEENEY

From The Paramount Motion Picture FORREST GUMP

FORREST GUMP - MAIN TITLE
(Feather Theme)

Eb ALTO SAXOPHONE
Band Arrangement

Music by ALAN SILVESTRI
Arranged by MICHAEL SWEENEY

From AN AMERICAN TAIL

**Words and Music by JAMES HORNER,
BARRY MANN and CYNTHIA WEIL**
Arranged by MICHAEL SWEENEY

Eb ALTO SAXOPHONE
Solo

MCA music publishing

FROM AN AMERICAN TAIL

SOMEWHERE OUT THERE

E♭ ALTO SAXOPHONE
Band Arrangement

Words and Music by JAMES HORNER,
BARRY MANN and CYNTHIA WEIL
Arranged by MICHAEL SWEENEY

Moderately Slow

MCA music publishing

From DANCES WITH WOLVES
THE JOHN DUNBAR THEME

By JOHN BARRY
Arranged by MICHAEL SWEENEY

E♭ ALTO SAXOPHONE
Solo

From **DANCES WITH WOLVES**
THE JOHN DUNBAR THEME

By **JOHN BARRY**
Arranged by MICHAEL SWEENEY

Eb ALTO SAXOPHONE
Band Arrangement

00860029

From The Paramount Motion Picture RAIDERS OF THE LOST ARK

RAIDERS MARCH

E♭ ALTO SAXOPHONE
Solo

By JOHN WILLIAMS
Arranged by MICHAEL SWEENEY

00860029

RAIDERS MARCH

Eb ALTO SAXOPHONE
Band Arrangement

By JOHN WILLIAMS
Arranged by MICHAEL SWEENEY

00860029

From APOLLO 13
APOLLO 13
(End Credits)

Eb ALTO SAXOPHONE
Solo

By JAMES HORNER
Arranged by MICHAEL SWEENEY

MCA music publishing

From APOLLO 13
APOLLO 13
(End Credits)

Eb ALTO SAXOPHONE
Band Arrangement

By JAMES HORNER
Arranged by MICHAEL SWEENEY

MCA music publishing

From The Universal Picture E.T. (THE EXTRA-TERRESTRIAL)

THEME FROM E.T. (THE EXTRA-TERRESTRIAL)

Eb ALTO SAXOPHONE
Solo

Music by JOHN WILLIAMS
Arranged by MICHAEL SWEENEY

MCA music publishing

THEME FROM E.T. (THE EXTRA-TERRESTRIAL)

Eb ALTO SAXOPHONE
Band Arrangement

Music by JOHN WILLIAMS
Arranged by MICHAEL SWEENEY

MCA music publishing

00860029

Theme From The Paramount Picture STAR TREK

Eb ALTO SAXOPHONE
Solo

Music by JERRY GOLDSMITH
Arranged by MICHAEL SWEENEY

00860029

STAR TREK® THE MOTION PICTURE

Eb ALTO SAXOPHONE
Band Arrangement

Music by JERRY GOLDSMITH
Arranged by MICHAEL SWEENEY

From The Universal Motion Picture BACK TO THE FUTURE

BACK TO THE FUTURE

E♭ ALTO SAXOPHONE
Solo

By ALAN SILVESTRI
Arranged by MICHAEL SWEENEY

MCA music publishing

E♭ ALTO SAXOPHONE
Band Arrangement

By ALAN SILVESTRI
Arranged by MICHAEL SWEENEY

MCA music publishing

00860029